The Joy of Drawing

BY GERHARD GOLLWITZER

Gramercy Publishing Company
New York

Originally published in West Germany © 1959 by Otto Maier
Verlag, under the title *Freude Durch Zeichnen*

Marginal drawing by Albrecht Dürer for Emperor Maximilian's Breviary. Original size.

CONTENTS

WHAT THIS BOOK AIMS TO DO 5

THE FIRST EXERCISES 9

WHY BEGIN SO STRANGELY? 11

SET YOUR BOUNDS 16

IMPORTANT RULES FOR DRAWING 21

LEARNING SELF-DISCIPLINE 24

DRAWING SURFACES AND MATERIALS 26

TRY OUT THE DRAWING MATERIALS 30

FIND BEAUTY IN DRAWING SURFACES 32

LEARN THE LANGUAGE OF DIRECTIONAL
  FORCES 36

MODULATE THE DRAWING SURFACE 40

STUDY PROPORTION 44

ALWAYS DRAW WITH YOUR EYES 47

MATTER IN SPACE 48

AN EYE FOR THE WHOLE AND FOR
  ESSENTIALS 53

ARCHITECTURAL FORM 56

PLANTS AND FLOWERS 70

FRUIT 82

TREES 85

WHAT IS "RIGHT"? 98

POINTERS FOR SELF-CRITICISM 100

FROM PRELIMINARY STUDY TO FINISHED
   PICTURE 104

LANDSCAPES 107

CONCLUSION 116

APPENDIX 117

INDEX 123

Translated by Dale and Margrete Cunningham

WHAT THIS BOOK AIMS TO DO

THIS BOOK AIMS to encourage you to draw. Everyone should draw, make music, write, and work creatively—these are things people need today. In the past, everyone took them for granted. The "folk" sang and invented dances, wove rugs and carved spoons—people were creative. Today, however, almost everyone is merely passive and receptive. Art books and photography have replaced the traveller's sketchbook and the paintbox, the metal industry has made the woodcarver's knife obsolete, and records and radios have banished the violin and singing voices.

But, once again people have been feeling the urge to be individually creative for the sake of feeling human—an urge often violently evoked by neuroses. A recent book by Karl Hils, "The Foundations of Human Craftsmanship", aims to lead you to the roots of human strength found in drawing, primarily because you are a human being and not a machine. The object is not on the paper, but in yourself; the goal is not your drawings, but you yourself. This is meant in the same sense as that of the Japanese master-archer who said: "The art of archery is not an athletic ability mastered more or less through primarily physical practice, but rather a skill with its origin in mental exercise and with its object consisting in mentally hitting the mark. Therefore, the archer is basically aiming for himself. Through this, perhaps, he will succeed in hitting the target—his essential self." (Herrigel). And when you have successful results, I hope you will not sink to bragging or start to think about selling while you are drawing. You would be cheating yourself of the most essential things, the best things:

intensifying your own feeling for life and enriching your experience. At the same time, the workers who are able to use what they have learned as an occupation are not forgotten—the gardener or the tailor, the craftsman or the scientist.

You can learn drawing in many ways and for many purposes. The method suggested here leads you from the elements of creative drawing to nature studies, to experiencing the wealth of the language of natural forms, to stimulating and enriching your imagination. Above all, you will become more adult or at least be on the verge of becoming more adult. These exercises have been developed from experience, and to encourage the beginner, the illustrations are largely student work. To be sure, they are frequently imperfect, but they are made by your peers. The illustrations are examples, suggestions pointing out the way.

What you see in exhibitions and magazines today may very well confuse you. Why should you still study nature in such an old-fashioned way in the age of photography? Why should you still render *objects* in an age of abstract painting? Why should you still delve so intensely into details, in the age of the impressionistic sketch? This book will treat such questions as they occur. At the beginning, however, it seems necessary to put these questions aside and just to start working. Then much will be answered by itself. One more thing: this is a *course* in drawing, not a *reader* about drawing. Only a person who does the exercises will understand it correctly. To be sure, the book cannot and does not attempt to be a substitute for a good teacher in person.

It is advisable in using the book to look the whole book through first, and always to read each chapter completely before occupying yourself with a new section of exercises. The greatest difficulty of this "long-distance teaching" is that the author has to divide a single large problem into individual sections, one following the other, whereas teaching in person is adjusted to the needs of the pupil. For example, the teacher can suggest working with more accuracy or with greater boldness according to the circumstances, or he can mix "abstract" exercises with a study of nature.

"Many roads lead to Rome"—towards seeing creatively and towards forming what you have seen creatively, not towards mannerisms aiming for "effects" or to an uninspired copy of nature. I hope to succeed in doing what the artist Paul Klee advised a teacher to do: "Let your pupils experience how a bud is formed and how a tree opens up so that they will become just as rich, just as flexible, and just as capricious as nature itself. Observation is a revelation, an insight into the workshop of creation. Therein lies the mysterious secret."

"Express Yourself in Drawing", a book by the same author and published by the same company, continues the stimulation started here and progresses to drawing portraits, figures and animals.

A WORD ABOUT THE ILLUSTRATIONS

UNIDENTIFIED PICTURES ARE the work of students, mostly in the author's classes. Most of the student artists were 20 to 23 years old.

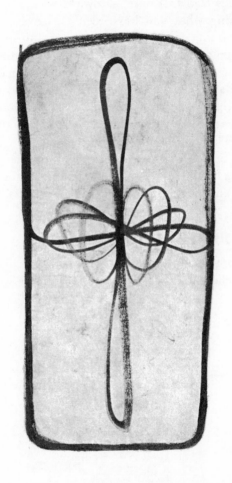

THE FIRST EXERCISES

USE CHEAP PAPER at the beginning—newsprint, inexpensive writing paper, or thin drawing paper. Get yourself a pad or substantial supply of large sheets about 12 in. x 16 in. so that your work can proceed without interruption. For the time being, use soft pencils, charcoal pencils or sticks, ball-point pens, or brushes for your drawing. Put a sheet (with a pad underneath for protection) on a table and *stand* in front of it: then you will work with more freedom than if you sat down.

Now, hovering over the paper like a bird of prey, draw a few squares with rounded corners in the air until you land with your pencil (or brush) on the paper. Don't lift the pencil from the paper, but let it continue long enough to get a real feeling of the square drawing surface. Then move towards the inside of the square with horizontal and vertical lines. Repeat these

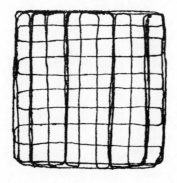

with broader and narrower spaces or with more verticals or more horizontals.

Starting the same way, draw a circle and then spiral inwards to the middle. On the next sheet, start in the middle and draw the spiral outwards, emphasizing the final circle by redrawing it several times. Let your pencil run along the inside edge of the circle in either large or small spirals. Always draw everything without lifting your pencil, and draw it boldly.

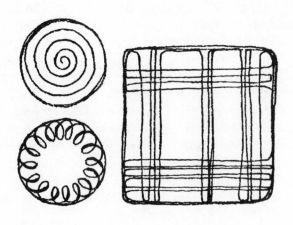

WHY BEGIN SO STRANGELY?

LET'S SUPPOSE that you have already drawn a lot. From experience we know that people, especially when they draw from nature, usually tend to become too picayune. Also, they are usually cramped when drawing. In addition, they take for granted those things which one first has to master: the drawing surface and drawing materials. Finally, they frequently only copy; that is, they reproduce only the *exterior* image and not the *essence* of objects.

These first exercises serve to make you bold, to loosen you up, and to let you master the drawing surface, the formats, the media, and the language of forms. Then later everything will go much easier and better. For best results, don't take these suggestions as assignments or exercises but rather as rules of the game. And don't look down on these games. Take part in them happily and let yourself be surprised by the thoughts that occur to you. Play like a child taking his game seriously, who does not *pretend* to be a mother or an engineer, but really

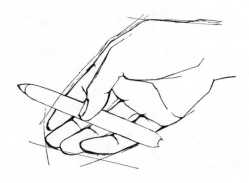

is this person, a child whose rules for the game are *rules for living.*

Always hold your pencil or brush loosely in your hand. Hold it with the ends of your fingers and with your thumb—that is, don't hold it as if you were writing. Always draw from the center of your body, from where guidance can be given, rather than from the wrist. The power should run from the center of your body through your shoulder and arm to the point of the pencil.

Conquer the Drawing Surface

Start as you did before and fill a square with diagonals and their parallels.

From circles you can progress to the figure 8, drawing both horizontal and vertical 8s. Develop figures out of them.

Fill circles with all different sorts of lines. Don't think them out beforehand, but instead invent them while your pencil is making the circle.

Working the same way, draw long rectangles or tall, narrow ones. Don't construct your rectangles out of four shaky lines

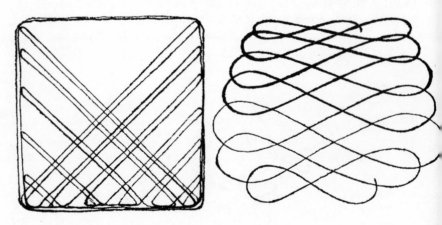

timidly set together. Instead, *form* them without lifting your pencil from the paper, always going round the corners without straining. Then emphasize these high or long outlines with interior horizontal or vertical lines so that the height seems even higher and the breadth even broader.

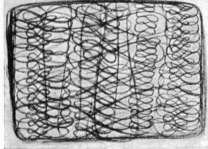

SET YOUR BOUNDS

AFTER YOU HAVE decided on a format and have the outline, set several points anywhere inside the outline and play around them so that you develop either areas of strength or empty spaces. After placing the points, return to the edge and redraw the outline before you start drawing inside the boundaries.

Create "obstacles" for yourself with definite exercises which restrain you from completely free play and thereby give your drawing sense and form. These exercises can be either abstract or representational. Here too, draw everything *without interruption*. If you have to stop for some reason, when you return to the exercise start again by redrawing the outline several times before you continue work on the interior.

The best exercises are those which form a contrast: static-dynamic, horizontal-vertical, thick-thin, large-small, empty-full, pointed-blunt, round-angular, concentrated-scattered.

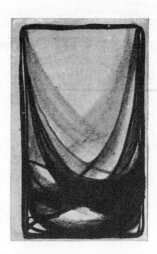

Think about appropriate contrasting motifs from nature: a seashore with poplars, a large pumpkin with many small grapes, or seashells among stones. However, first "translate" the representational theme into a formal theme. Don't just draw the poplars or fruit but rather create a composition: set the horizontal of the water against the towering forms of the poplars, the large globe of the pumpkin against the small balls of the

grapes, the elongated ovals of the shells against the small
round forms of the stones. Or let a city—that is, varied squares
—rise along a slope above a river, represented by horizontal

lines. It can be bounded by rolling hills and overlaid with Zeppelins of clouds.

Outline a tall, thin rectangle and then draw *with both hands*. Start in the middle of the base and draw up toward the center. Open out to both sides with small circles or large, rising ovals. Or else start at the bottom with standing and lying ovals, rise toward the center, and finish with small circles and ovals to the right and left at the top. While you are doing this, you can think vaguely about trees or flowers.

IMPORTANT RULES FOR DRAWING

NEVER LOSE AN overall view of the whole sheet. You should look at the sheet from as vertical a position as possible. It is therefore advisable either to lean the drawing surface against the edge of a table and hold it on your knees, or to lay it on a table with a rising slant, or to work at an easel. *Always leave your body free to move and keep your distance from the sheet.*

As a support for the paper you can use a drawing board, a piece of fiberboard, or some heavy cardboard. Fasten the paper with thumbtacks (drawing pins) or clips; it has to lie smooth. You should not make your work harder by having to fight loose or wavy paper or poor drawing materials. Never roll paper unnecessarily. Paper that has been rolled up can easily be smoothed out. Lay it on a table so that it curls away from the table top. Then press it flat or pull it down tautly over the edge of the table.

Do not work *too small*; it is better to draw small things enlarged. And, at first, always leave yourself a margin about two or three fingers wide. You will find a need for it often enough.

Start with light, boldly sketched strokes and hold your pencil in the way described on page 12. In general, draw loosely; don't "dig in".

At the *beginning*, always have the *end* in sight; with the detail in mind, think of the whole. One good bit of advice: when you are drawing the head of a figure, look at the feet, and when you are drawing the feet, look at the head.

A drawing should be *finished in every stage of completion*. It

Detail from Albrecht Dürer's "The Flight to Egypt." Woodcut, 15″.

should grow from a large totality into the richer, more detailed parts. Never lose yourself in the details and never start with them. Therefore, stand off and look at your drawing from a distance again and again while you are working, or else look at it in a mirror or by turning the drawing upside down.

At the outset, always draw in all those non-existent lines which contribute to the clarification of the forms. You continually have to visualize an idea of the totality.

Every stroke must *say* something. Do not mistake a line which suggests, for one which is merely approximate. Even something which seems restlessly disordered (like the surface of a ball of wool, a maze of wire, or a meadow) should not be rendered chaotically but rather should be formed. *Drawing something entangled does not mean to draw it disorderly.* You can see that here from Dürer's palm leaves.

LEARNING SELF-DISCIPLINE

Now YOU SHOULD repeat everything previously learned more consciously and more exactly. But don't lose the swing of things doing this. The principle of doing everything with a big bold stroke is still valid. The corners should now be angular, the spaces in a checkerboard division of a square regular, and the circles more exact and less like potatoes or plums. It is still important to stand there with your concentrated strength and to draw with your whole body from its center. Don't "stammer" while you are drawing.

Make use of your breath in this way: first whistle out; then just wait to breathe in until the air is forced into you *of its own accord*; don't breathe in; don't help it along with your muscles; just let the air breathe itself in. Now hold your breath a bit and start to draw with the flow of breathing-out.

You should devote special attention to the S-curve. Start in a rectangle with two half-circles. Redraw them a few times in order to get the feel of the pleasant, uniform curves. Then give them some tension: let them stretch out flatter or curve more sharply. Now apply the principle to a letter. Draw a large letter in either a long or tall rectangle, and intensify it with additional lines. They can either emphasize the flow of the letter with parallels or increase the tension of the curves.

Another application: invent profiles out of S-curves with different tensions. Let the most varied profiles *occur* to you while drawing, and don't try to rack your brains for the profiles of definite people.

DRAWING SURFACES AND MATERIALS

THE MEDIUM HAS an active effect on the final results. Drawing does not start with the first stroke on the paper, but rather with the choice of materials. Drawing materials are not interchangeable like handkerchiefs. Consequently, I prefer to talk about the materials for drawing than about techniques. Technique sounds so impersonal and objective, it easily creates the wrong impression—makes you think you can draw the same way with a pen or with charcoal. Photographs and halftone illustrations which make everything equally smooth and equally black have dulled our eyes to the varied, sensual language of different sorts of papers and tools. Actually, there is no single, universal drawing surface. Each paper has a definite surface and a certain shade of white tending either towards grey or yellow. Likewise, there is no single drawing stroke, but rather lines made with a pointed stiff pen or lines drawn with a soft brush. Here is a survey of the most important materials.

1. PAPER: We distinguish between smooth and rough paper, between sized and absorbent, grained and stippled, heavy and thin. Collect and try out different papers, everything from paper napkins to the precious hand-made Japanese papers. Everyone quickly finds his special favorites. Primarily, you need three types of drawing paper. First of all, you need a lot of inexpensive "scrap paper" for exercises and sketches, something like newsprint. Secondly, you need either single sheets or pads of good drawing paper (with a plate finish for pen). A pretty, somewhat rough paper for use with charcoal, reed pen, or brush is "Ingres paper", which can be purchased in all

shades. Third, you need a pocket-sized sketchbook—this you can easily get or make for yourself.

2. PENCILS: There are many degrees of hardness, which are indicated by a standard code. H, 2H, 3H, and so on indicate increasing degrees of hardness; B, 2B, 3B, etc. show increasing softness; and HB is medium hard. For the first exercises, a soft drawing pencil between 2B and 4B is best. Later you can use HB. There are also "drawing leads", that is, leads which fit into special adjustable lead holders and are always ready to use. For fine work, however, the traditional wooden pencil is preferable. The paper has to have "tooth" enough (a sufficiently rough surface) so that the pencil will leave a mark, and the surface must be hard enough so that the pencil does not dig into it. The blackness and density of a stroke depend on the paper. The same pencil will write dark on grainy paper and grey on smooth paper. But don't try to achieve too much depth by gouging into the paper. For bold drawing, a large-lead carbon or charcoal pencil is recommended—it can be used either pointed or on the broad side.

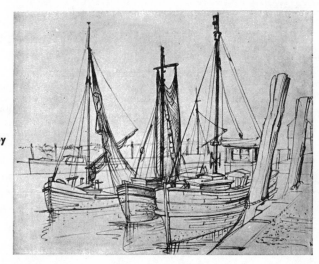

Pen drawing by student.

3. CHARCOAL: This is a soft material appropriate for shaded drawings. A charcoal line is deep, velvety black, and dull even in the deepest layers. Such a line is much coarser than that of a pencil, but it has a greater range from black to light grey. However, charcoal all too easily leads one astray into pretentiousness and smearing. Charcoal can be bought in wooden holders or as long square sticks. It is better to use the sticks; you can break them into pieces a half-inch to an inch long and use the corners for line work, the sides for large areas. Sanguine (a red crayon) and sepia (brown) are similar to charcoal.

4. FIXATIVE: Since soft pencil and charcoal are easily smeared, they have to be "fixed". A good fixative is a 5% solution of white, bleached shellac in alcohol. You can buy it ready to use, either in bottles or spray cans. Apply it carefully at a distance of about 12 to 18 inches from the drawing. It is better to spray several thin coats of fixative rather than one heavy coat, since drops or little puddles leave ugly spots. First try a few test sprays into the air. If you are using a bottle with a mouth-type atomizer, the less fixative in the bottle the harder it will be to apply, because the liquid has to be drawn up by the flow of air.

5. PENS: There are fine, pointed drawing nibs as well as the usual writing pen points. It is also interesting to work with homemade reed and goose-quill pens. *How to make them:* Take a sturdy, dry reed with a node at one end and cut it off close to the next node. Bevel off the end with a very sharp knife and clean out the pith. Then lay the point on a hard support with the inside down, clip off the end at an angle to the outside, and split the nib exactly in the middle with the point of your knife, going from the inside to the end. Insert a narrow, ✓-shaped strip of metal into the reed to hold the ink on the underside of the pen. You treat a goose-quill the same way. Both types have to be resharpened frequently, but the little effort needed is worth the results. For the first exercises, a "Rapidograph" pen or even a ball-point pen (which ruins

modern handwriting) is good. With either of these, as is not possible with a pen, you can draw in all directions, backwards and forwards, without picking up.

6. INKS: We distinguish between ordinary, thin writing inks and the heavier, waterproof drawing or India inks. The new Pelikan India ink for use in fountain pens, a black ink, can be recommended.

7. BRUSHES: For your work at the beginning, two brushes are enough: a small one about size #5, and a larger one about size #12. You can paint with ink, India ink, diluted ink, or watercolors. When buying brushes, be sure that the brush bristles do not split apart or open up when they are wet; instead they should form a fine point. They should not be jammed down on the points or left standing overnight in a glass of water. Clean your brushes as soon as you have finished using them.

8. ERASERS: There are regular pencil erasers, ink and typewriter erasers, gum erasers, and kneaded erasers. Kneaded erasers are used for soft pencil and charcoal. First you dab at the spot, then carefully rub it, and finally remove the remainder with an ordinary eraser. Inked lines can also be erased with a razor blade, but be careful not to scrape a hole through the paper. Use an eraser as little as possible at the beginning.

A final word: Besides using black on white, you can also draw with white on black or with black and white on tinted papers.

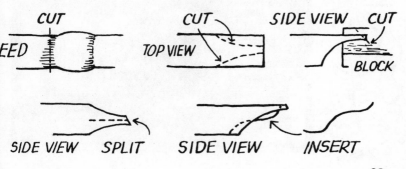

TRY OUT THE DRAWING MATERIALS

AFTER THE LAST chapter you may well be afraid of the vast variety of materials—and that was only a small selection! But you will soon know your way around after you have played the worthwhile game of trying out the possibilities. If you cannot wait to draw a plant or a building, you might just as well take a photograph right away. For, after all, drawing is not merely reproducing something visible but experiencing deeper intellectual and spiritual joys. Therefore, grant yourself a few hours to try out different media on various papers until you have found your favorites.

The illustrations on this and the next page should show what fun you can have trying out the media. Often the games take form of their own accord. (Below) charcoal. (Left) steel pen. (Opposite page) goosequill pen, steel pen, reed pen, brush, fine drawing pen.

FIND BEAUTY IN DRAWING SURFACES

CONTINUE YOUR EXERCISES in the language of drawing by trying to bring out through the drawing media the essential substance of various objects.

Start by inventing different modes of expression with a pen by filling up two-inch squares with dots, checks, curlicues, wavy lines, circles, and latticed or pulsing lines. Put all sorts of really dissimilar things together—a piece of wire screen, a feather, a piece of bark, a polished knife—and study the charm of the surface of each one. Observe the different kinds of bark

Enlarged details from engravings by Dürer. (Above) From "Mary and the Locusts," 2½". (Left) From "The Prodigal Son," 3½".

in the woods. Study striped, spotted, or speckled animals and the shagginess or sleekness of their fur. Observe the glossy, ribbed, or thready structure of cloth. Use your sense of feeling —touch the cracked or polished surfaces, the wrinkled or taut ones. Direct your attention only to these things, and forget about the contours and mass of the objects as well as light and shade.

Draw a number of uniform objects, that is, objects which are scarcely different in contour but which are decidedly different in surface texture; for example, an apple, a lemon or an orange, an egg, a rubber ball, a marble, and an onion. Then draw a "still life" of things which contrast greatly, like feathers and glass on a screen, or a shaving brush and keys on a woven mat.

Then, after the pen, try out the same exercises with other media—pencil, charcoal, brush. You will discover that there is an especially suitable medium for each type of surface. But, on the other hand, you will also discover that the language of each drawing medium has an abundance of various possibilities, of vowels and consonants, so to speak.

In connection with this chapter also look at the illustrations on pages 22, 62, 64 (bottom), 65 (top), 66, 67, 76, 77 (right), 88, 93 and 113.

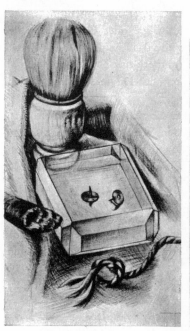

Student drawings. (Left) Pencil. (Below) Steel pen.

Enlarged detail from Dürer engraving, "Saint Eustace," 6″.

LEARN THE LANGUAGE
OF DIRECTIONAL FORCES

AT THE START you think you know what an object looks like. There it is: you see it. You sit down in front of it and start to make a drawing of it. Then difficulties arise and you try to save yourself by sketching even more precisely, continuing this process to its bitter end.

Let's do it another way here. Ask yourself: How does a tree speak? What do its forms have to tell? And: How do I use the language of drawn forms to say what I have felt and observed? In the wintertime a tree speaks through the flow of its branches and the filigree work they form. In the spring it is by means of the little leaves dotted onto the filigree. In the summer the tree speaks with the bulkiness of the foliage cresting it. Each type of tree has its own dialect just as each individual tree has its own manner of speaking.

The farther you come in your work, the better you will understand why the attitude described in the beginning is in error. The more surprises you experience, the more you discover out of doors and in yourself, and the more questions that come up, the more you will realize that you do not know what things *really* look like. When he was an old man, the great philosopher Socrates said, "I know that I know nothing." In the same way, the older he gets, every great artist says, "I see that I see nothing, that the manifestations which seemed to lie so visibly before my eyes at the beginning are miracles which I marvel at more and more."

An extensive program of work must be divided into small exercise units. You have to cut a cake into pieces to be able to eat it. An adult can tell the time just from the position of a clock's hands, but as a child he had to learn slowly from looking at the clock's numbers. Certainly you can still remember how your teacher taught you writing and arithmetic in sections, one after the other. You don't think about that any

Chinese woodcut copy of a wash drawing from "The Textbook of a Mustard-Seed Garden." 10″. The experiences of these expressive rhythms, done from imagination, of course, were created with brush, pencil, carbon pencil, and charcoal. Open your eyes to this abundance wherever you go. Your drawing will help you do it.

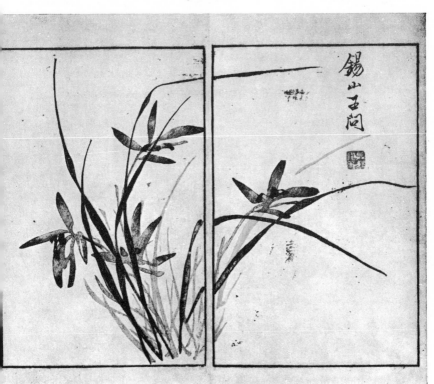

more when you write today. In the same way, everything you now practice in individual exercises will soon sum up to an understandable whole.

Let's turn now to the language of lines, of directed forces. Start again with a square and let truly different kinds of leafless trees *occur* to you. Do not draw the botanical aspects of oaks, poplars, or weeping willows; instead, invent tree forms —one with a stiffly ascending trunk and one with a flexible, irregularly gnarled trunk, one with branches stretching out broadly or straining pertly upwards or hanging down smoothly or with feathery branches.

Fill up a broad oblong format playfully with tree rhythms which really contrast to each other.

39

MODULATE THE DRAWING SURFACE

UP TO NOW you have been working primarily with lines. Now you should become acquainted with the tonal media and the language of toned areas on the drawing surface. For this purpose use charcoal without a holder or a large brush with some water color or with ink and water. You can use non-absorbent drawing paper as well as absorbent paper for a drawing surface or even newsprint or strong paper napkins. Begin again with the outline of a square or a rectangle and make the surface vibrate with light and dark tones.

One time try going from the outside to the inside, getting lighter until you have an untouched spot of the original paper in the middle. Or start at the top with dark, horizontal stripes and let them get lighter until you have a white stripe in the middle; then let them get dark again towards the bottom edge.

You will soon notice that the danger is in making *everything* too light or *everything* too dark. Then there is no true modulation and the tones swim into each other. Therefore, you have to divide the modulation clearly into three or four steps, just as you have to learn the individual tones of a melody in exact intervals in order to be able to sing the stream of the melody without slurring. Distinguish, therefore, between black, dark grey, medium grey, light grey, and white. It is important that each tone touches the next one *without* a black dividing line and *without* even a tiny white strip between them.

As is done in a striped textile pattern, place clearly graduated stripes of varying width and varying tone next to each other, always in the same sequence. This forces you to pay close attention to the tonal values. For this exercise you can divide your strip (about three inches high) lightly with a pencil. You can also divide your sheet into a checkerboard pattern as in the first exercises and then fill the squares in with tones. Or draw large and small moons with shaded halos in a black sky. Or take the inside of a pine forest as a stimulus in order to form a chiaroscuro vision of richly shaded trunks. (A chiaroscuro sketch uses only light and shade, omitting any colors.) However, don't draw pine trees yet and don't try to *model* the trunks either; instead *modulate* the surface with variously shaded stripes.

The better you have tuned your eyes to the "sound" of the tonal gradations, the better you will employ the gradations with expression and certainty. These examples of student drawings are (above) charcoal on tinted paper, (below left) charcoal, (below right) brush. All were done without the aid of a preliminary sketch.

During these exercises, pay attention to light and shade everywhere in nature, and study the intervals of the tones. Do not see any boundary lines, but rather only areas of tones, only shades. Notice the graceful, weightless silvery nuances of a foggy morning, the strong contrasts at high noon, or the tension at night between the brightness of a house door, the semi-darkness of the wall, and the blackness of the sky.

In this connection also look at the illustrations on pages 49, 52, 63, 69, 79 (below), 97, 103 (below), 108, 109 and 112.

STUDY PROPORTION

GETTING A FEELING for proportion, for the relation of the parts to the whole and of the parts to each other, must become part of your flesh and blood. Here we will draw tulips in three equal-sized rectangles. Remember the first games, and at the start let your hand hover over the sheet like a bird until the pencil settles into an outline that starts gently and becomes increasingly stronger. Now let your pencil rise vertically into the middle of the rectangle from the middle of the lower edge, opening up into a flower cup. Let this calyx fill exactly half the format of the picture on the first sheet, a third of the format on the second, and two-thirds on the third. Compare your sheets with each other, and note the proportion of cup to stem.

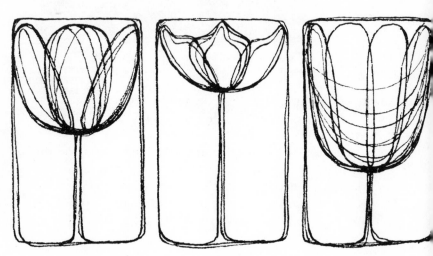

Note the same proportions of various wineglasses, as well as the relation of the breadth to the height. "Design" your own wineglasses with really contrasting proportions, drawing them on the reverse side of silhouette paper and then cutting them out.

Study proportions wherever you go. In the facade of a house, for example, note the relation of the width to the height, of the height of the windows to the height of the building, of the foundation-work height to the height of the house. Compare different facades. Which is more "beautiful"—which "sounds" better? Compare the height of a tree to that of its crown. Or compare the three parts of a face: the forehead, the nose, and the mouth-chin part. Compare a slender boy to a fat man with short legs, a slim girl to a plump matron. Compare the relationship of head to body with a one-year-old child, a six-year-old, and a man. How many times does the head go into the length of the body? Let the expressive language of proportions everywhere have its effect on you.

"Sighting" will sharpen your eye for proportions, for conscious understanding and comprehension of relationships. For this, hold a long pencil or a stick or rod like an umbrella in your hand; stretch your arm out horizontally with the stick held vertically; now line up the end of the rod with the highest point of the object to be measured—that is, get your eye, the end of the stick, and the upper limit of the object in a straight line. Then run your thumbnail so far down the rod that your eye, your thumbnail, and the lowest point of the object are also lined up.

By the "sighting" method of measurement you can take the dimensions of the whole thing. For example, with the measure of the foundation-work you can determine the height of the whole building. How many times does the part go into the whole? What is the proportion of the parts to each other?

With horizontal measurements, repeat the same process but from left to right. What is the relation of the width to the height? To be sure, when you are "sighting", you always have to stand on the same spot and keep your arm stretched out. The slightest change causes large errors.

Practice your feeling for proportions with this method, but do *not* use it for the following exercises. It is frequently misunderstood and misused; and it all too easily misleads you to mechanical *copying*, distracting you from creating. In any case, if you ever should use "sighting" of the comparative dimensions as a help—as a self-check and as encouragement in order to perceive the greater, more definite tension in nature—then do it only *after* you have sketched the whole thing.

In conclusion, a saying from Dürer: "Correct proportion results in good form, not only in a painting, but in all things —however they may be produced."

ALWAYS DRAW WITH YOUR EYES

Do NOT WORK out your exercises only on paper; practice with your eyes continually, wherever you are. Generally our sight has become superficial and flighty, as our eyes only slip over objects and pictures. Quick-changing impressions on the street, flat photographs in magazines, and the flickering cinema have made us almost blind and deaf to the unobstrusive language of lines, forms, tones, and proportions. To be a creative artist means to hear the language of forms, to understand it, and to express yourself in it.

Even if you do not become an artist, through your drawing you can share a little in the artistic way of living, or rejoicing, of growing. "The painter is the *confidant* of nature. Flowers carry on dialogues with him through the graceful bending of their stems and the harmoniously tinted nuances of their blossoms. Every flower is a cordial word which nature directs towards him." (Rodin). Then too there is no longer such a thing as annoying "bad" weather. "There is nothing more festive than to walk through the woods on a gloomy morning like today, when the rain is falling straight down and drips from leaf to leaf and from needle to needle, when one is treading silently on the soft ground through a green depth which iridesces all about in silvery tints and in cool emerald preciousness." (Scheffler)

Another time you may trace along a graceful birch branch with your eyes or the tortured, jerky zigzag of an apple tree. You will notice tension and strength or fatigue and slackness in handwriting. You will have the experience that until now you had not known how the world looks even though you had believed that liar, photography. Your eye becomes creative again. It is *always* drawing-lesson time, even if you are not drawing.

MATTER IN SPACE

You can experience a new way of discovering your surroundings primarily through your senses. Walk through rooms consciously, through doorways, down the stairs, stroll through a church, cross a broad square. While you are walking, feel the open space with your body, feel the narrowness of an alley. Get a feeling as if your own body were a column in space. This may sound odd, but it is gradually becoming accepted that such sensual experiences are as necessary for us as our daily bread—indispensable to save us from becoming mere systematic, rationalistic machine men.

Then, what you have experienced on a large scale, playfully repeat on a small scale. Play with matchboxes, building blocks, spools, and the like. Make buildings, streets, and

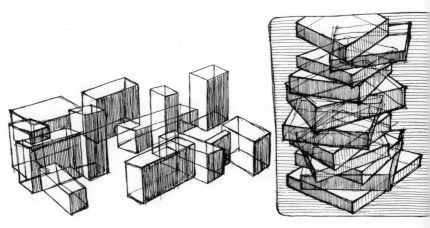

squares with them as children do. Add a pencil or a little bottle for a tower.

Look at your child's game from all sides; go for a walk in it with your eyes like a pygmy. Then draw it from your imagination. That is, go to another table and draw simple diagonally placed pictures, *not* the matchboxes and blocks, but rather the cubic bodies and the spaces they form. First, draw horizontal lines in your rectangle with your pencil or ball-point pen to represent the ground level, to make the base materially visible on your paper. Then build up the cubes from the base. First draw the ground-plan, then the verticals in the corners, and finally the flat "roofs". Always draw the unseen parts along with the rest. And just attack it happily; you are capable of

49

doing it by now. The "beauty" of the drawing is not important yet—only the creation and forming of matter and space.

Go to your play-table again—two boxes and a piece of cardboard across the top—a bench. Draw the bench from several sides, then three or four benches like it, add a table, a pole, put a sunshade on top, and continue letting your fantasy work like this. Try it with a heap of books or a pile of suitcases. "Shade" everything by hatching, that is, only with lines which indicate the directions: vertical, horizontal, or slanting to the right or to the left. Never think about perspective or giving the illusion of space. When you have done this two or three times, you can also use tones as illustrated on page 49.

Round forms can be added quite naturally: cylinders, cones, and spheres—that is, columns, towers, and smokestacks.

Think up flowers in this manner: top off leaves with their calyxes, cups, or overlapping petals. And trees: cones for fir trees, balls for beeches, cylinders for poplars.

Observe yourself to see if—completely unintentionally and without thinking specifically about it—your surroundings do not strike you now as being more concrete, more "cubistic". Notice whether or not you see forces everywhere to which you were previously blind.

There is no sense in looking backwards romantically and saying, "Dürer didn't do exercises like this." He lived in a completely different era. Sensual experience and genuine creativity were at that time still in *everyone's* blood, in everyone's vision. You have only to look at a farmhouse or a page of a community registry-book or a forged-iron cross from that time. They were not designed by specialists, by artists, architects, commercial artists or skilled artisans, but they are still works of art. When a draughtsman of that time drew a plant for a scientific work (and therefore was not drawing a "piece of art"), he preceded this work with perception and experiencing of the object. He created with the genuine means of creation: with lines, tones, color, rhythms, relationships, contrasts, and forms.

51

He did not photograph nature with his pencil. It is for this reason that people today are able to hang such prints on the wall, framed as works of art—something that will certainly never happen with the illustrations in the natural science textbooks of today.

Student drawing, charcoal.

AN EYE FOR THE WHOLE
AND FOR ESSENTIALS

WHEN YOU BEGIN to draw from nature you should be ready
to use everything which you have learned. To set an object
in front of you and to start drawing immediately betrays a
false diligence. How should you start then? Look at the subject
as if you had never seen it before. Examine it from every side,
draw its outline with your eyes or in the air with your hands,
and saturate yourself with it. Absorb it as a *totality.*

The object has to become a "motif", an inducement to
action; it should not remain a "model". Search out such
motifs for yourself.

Let's take a pine branch as an example. Look at the whole
form and its decisive directions. Distinguish between the
important and the unimportant. Then, through your eyes,

This is one of the most important chapters! Look at these illustrations with your eyes open only a slit in order not to let yourself be confused by the details. Compare the pine branch here (charcoal) with the illustrations on page 78, in which the work started here is carried on a step further.

absorb the essence of the motif. In this case, you will find it is the stretching, bristly, pine-tree quality. But, then, don't make a copy of the pine branch. Instead draw it from your sensed conception of it—*par coeur*, as the French say. In the same way, hunt up one after the other; a slender poplar, a stunted fruit tree, a sunflower, a chestnut. Don't say it is too hard. It is only hard to draw what has not passed through your heart.

Therefore, always take into consideration that in art *the whole is more than the sum of its parts*. A tree is more than the sum of its branches and leaves ranked one after another. Secondly, discover the form-language of the objects: with a plant, it is what speaks to the eyes and through the eyes and not the botanical aspects. Observe the crammed-full quality of a chestnut, the tortuous prickliness of a thistle, or the slim gracefulness of a birch.

In addition to the pictures on the opposite page, also look at the illustrations on pages 64 (below), 65 (above), 68 (above), 108, 109 and 112 (below).

ARCHITECTURAL FORM

FIRST STUDY *angular objects*. Draw freehand an outline of the base, a side view, and various diagonal views of a cube and a matchbox.

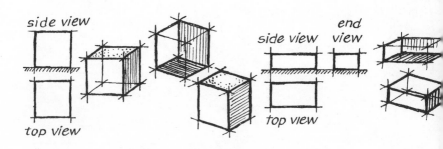

Place two or three matchboxes in all sorts of arrangements, and draw the outlines and diagonal views of many such combinations.

Put roofs on cube "houses", a tent-shaped roof and a span-roof. Then put a span-roof and a hip-roof on houses with rectangular ground-plans. You will notice that even with such simple exercises you have to proceed slowly, step by step, *always from the bottom to the top*—from the ground or from the base of the roof, whichever the case may be. Notice the guide lines in the illustrations.

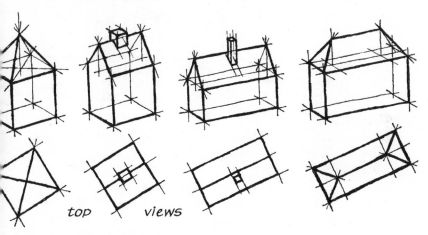

top *views*

Draw simple furniture: a table with two chairs or a chest of drawers on legs. Then a house with a roof, stairs, a balcony, chimneys, doors, and windows. The more cautiously and faith-

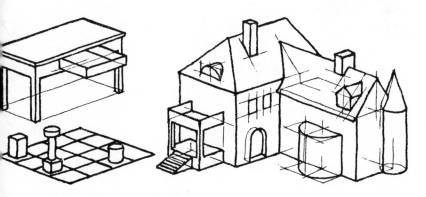

fully you proceed and the more calculations you make during the process, the more quickly—not the more slowly—it will go.

Fold a few strips of paper and set them up in front of you. Draw them directly and draw them from memory.

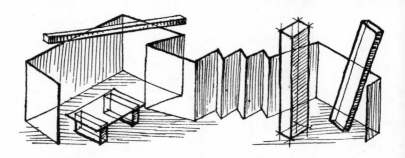

Draw children's building blocks, wooden joints, scaffolding, stairs, and similar objects.

Now proceed to *round forms*. Seen from an angle, the circular outlines of the forms become ovals. Be careful not to make them look like squares with rounded corners or like plum pits. Perhaps it is preferable to practice this in advance by first drawing a square (seen from an angle) which would fit around the circle, and then drawing the oval into this. Notice in the illustration where and how the curves nestle up to the straight lines.

Begin by drawing the basic forms of the most important geometrical figures in base, side, and diagonal views. Always start with the central axis. Draw these basic figures with six to eight cross-sections.

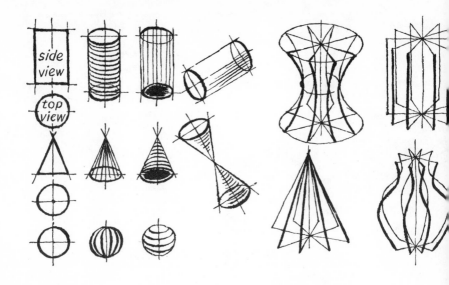

Draw bottles both standing and lying down, a cylindrical coffee pot with a handle, spout, and a knob on the cover, and a teacup with a handle. Draw piles of barrels or pipes.

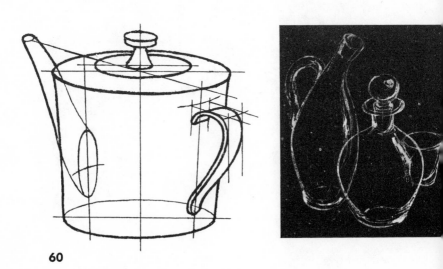

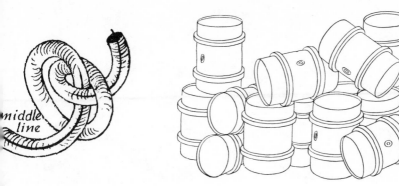

Draw gears and notched beams.

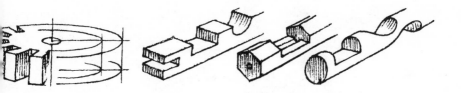

Draw rolled-up strips of paper, wood shavings, and rolls of wallpaper. Then snail shells, knotted strings, and entwined snakes. Don't forget the guiding line through the middle of the cross-section. Draw all these things from nature as well as from your imagination.

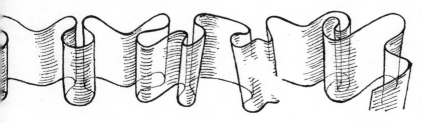

Draw a crown of thorns from memory, a woven fence, a wicker basket, a key ring, or a carpet beater.

"Osier Baskets," charcoal, by Fritz Griebel.

Combine round and angular figures as in the house on page 57.

Draw your room from memory along with the most important furniture. Draw a house constructed of several parts, a gate with the adjoining houses, a garden archway.

A few rules: Always start from the ground up, like an architect. A beginner is apt to be much more interested in the gables and neglect the foundations of the house. Second, always proceed from the most important points to those of secondary importance. The beginner likes to lose himself too quickly in details—windows or balconies—and neglects the more important things, namely, the main structure of the building. Third, look at every object from all sides at the start, penetrate into it, and become intimately acquainted with it. Fourth, draw a great deal from imagination and little from nature—

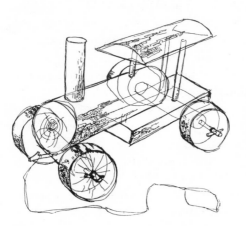

Both these exercises, when they are examined, show what has to happen in every drawing: first, the grasp of the whole, then the detail work. (Above) white chalk and charcoal. (Left) steel pen.

All these exercises are now united in this pen drawing of a carpenter's workbench, done by a 15-year-old. Of course, even this is drawn from imagination.

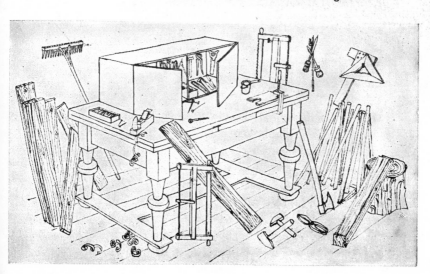

The illustrations on these and the next pages show pen drawings of buildings and interiors. In one case, more emphasis is put on the structural aspects; in the next, more on the form of the space. (Above) Rudolf Niess, "The Norder Gate in Flensburg," pen, original size.

but even when you do have a model, draw from the imagination as well. You should not try for "views"—which can be photographed more quickly and more exactly—but for a created form, which only an artist can make. It is the purpose of these exercises to keep true, creative construction of forms apart from views mechanically projected onto the paper.

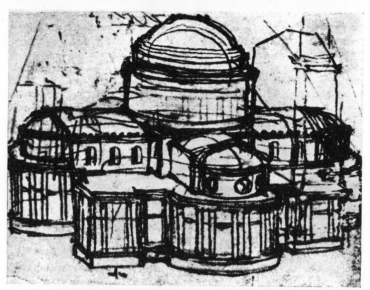

(Above)   Working sketch in pen, by Leonardo da Vinci.

Draw, or, to be more accurate, paint vases and buildings with a broad brush and without making a preliminary pencil drawing. Pay attention to the tonal values. The outlines of the forms should be created by chiaroscuro and not drawn in with lines.

PLANTS AND FLOWERS

LET'S PROCEED FROM man-made objects to nature. Remember that flowers, plants, trees, and the landscape all have to become part of your inner self before you draw them. Try to feel as if you were a tree before drawing it. This sounds strange again, but when you try it out, you will see what is meant.

Today's city dweller is very unaccustomed to nature; he probably gets into the fields and woods only on weekends. But in order really to be able to draw grass and flowers, you have to have lain in a field, seen the "forest" of grass undulating over you, smelled the field and the earth, and felt the sun. Look at flowers until they look back at you. Max Liebermann, the painter, said, "Love is everything in art. You can't paint anything without love; you can't even draw a blade of grass if you don't love it." An apple wants you to take it in your hand, to feel its taut curves with your hand, to smell its fragrance, and to taste its flesh.

So many modern human beings consciously have to make up as adults what our grandparents experienced directly and subconsciously as boys and girls. Don't think that this is a waste of time if you want to learn how to *draw*. It is exactly something of this quality which has to permeate your drawing. If you don't go into the fields and woods, then at least bring grass blades, flowers, and tree branches into your room and observe them frequently in peace and quiet before you draw them.

In any case, don't draw "corpses". When you pick a plant, it begins to die. When you get home, give it plenty of water and wait for it to recover completely, because the tautness of

the plant is supposed to stimulate tautness in you. Always set it up as it grew in nature, fastening it to the edge of a vase if you have to. Tree branches especially must stand before you exactly as they did in nature, even though this is frequently hard to arrange. An even better solution is to dig up the roots along with the plants.

Remember what was said in "An Eye for the Whole and for Essentials". Cover whole sheets helter-skelter from top to bottom with the language of tree and plant leaves: with spiny, broad, notched, or round forms; with rosettes, panicles, umbels, and clusters. Do the same with branches and bunches of pointed, oval, or serrated leaves. Draw them out-of-doors during a walk and draw them at home. Collect them in your heart as an amazed observer, not in a herbarium like a botanist. Invent characteristic signs for the oak, beech, and weeping willow. In this connection, look at the illustrations on pages 22, 33 (right) and 71.

Invent your own flower shapes—play the creator—and then go out and see what sort of things there really are of this type.

After this, study individual flowers exactly. They are not mere delicate "poems" but solid, material structures. However, don't get stuck here on your way to "perceptual creativity" and don't confuse our advice with cheap recipes for a technique of exact reproduction or for technical construction.

Draw all sorts of flower forms from your imagination—shapes like cups, bells, or plates. (See the illustrations, page 51.)

While doing this, always hatch according to the forms so that the hatching clarifies the form and so that you are building up the form with each line. The guide lines should not disturb you; in fact, they show what you understood during the work process. Also draw studies like this from nature, but bigger than life.

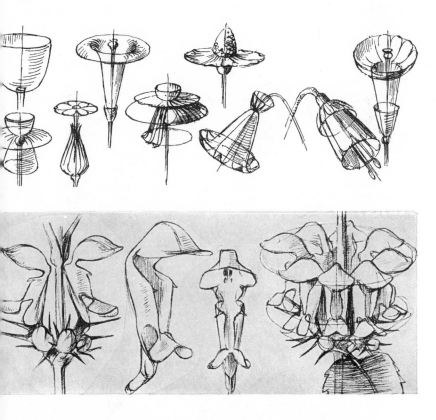

After this, when you venture to draw a whole plant or a bouquet, begin boldly with the main directions and dimensions. Compare the proportions of the size of the central groups and of the spaces between them. Notice how the parts are crowded together in one spot and have more than enough room in another, and how the intervals alternate rhythmically. Consider which part you will give the main emphasis, to which part you will then subordinate the others. From the whole, proceed slowly to the details. With leaves, go from the central vein over the rough outline to the smaller veins and to the characterization of the edges. Pay attention to how the leaf stems are attached to the stalks. And "learn to be industrious rather than fast" (Leonardo). See the illustrations below and on pages 37, 80 and 81.

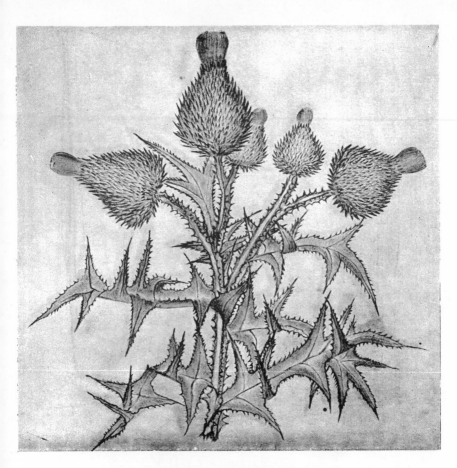

This 7″ pencil drawing was done by a 16-year-old.

This 9″ pencil drawing of a thistle is more complex and detailed than the one on the previous page. However, no clarity has been lost.

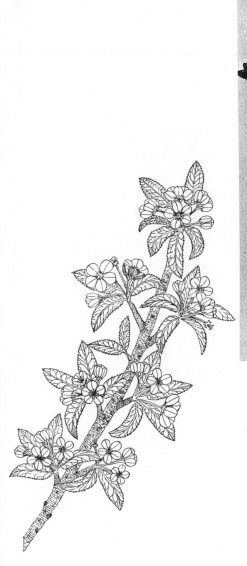

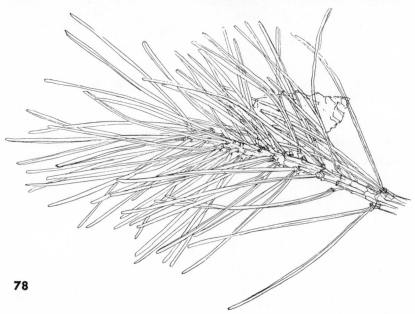

78

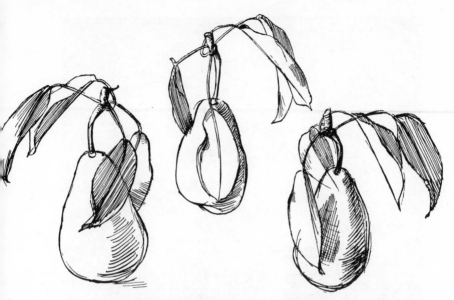

The same pear drawn from different views, with a ball-point pen. Notice the rhythm of the directional forces and the intervals.

Then also draw grasses and flowers with a brush, using absorbent paper without making a preliminary sketch. Try to realize the various widths and different tones with strong pressure on the brush. Nothing can be corrected, so it has to be right the first time.

FRUIT

THIS IS AN especially gratifying exercise: acorns with their little cups, pine cones, warm brown chestnuts with their prickly green shells burst partially or completely open! The fruits of the orchard—cherries, pears, and apples! A small branch with leaves and fruit on the tree out in the garden or a bowl full of fruit in the house! A half-peeled apple with the strip of peel still hanging on it and spiralling around itself! An orange with

the peel cut back so that the fruit is resting in a six- or eight-sided rosette! And finally vegetables: radishes, onions with a few layers of skin peeled off, cabbages. Also draw the fruits with many cross-sections as you did with the round forms previously. Touch them and "grasp" them so that you understand the language of their forms.

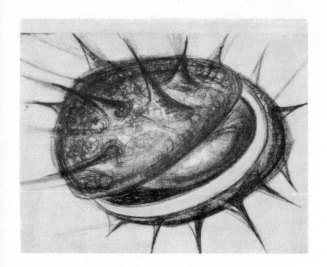

TREES

IN HIS *Green Henry* Gottfried Keller tells the story of how his
drawing of a tree began dashingly and ended wretchedly. A
gigantic beech tree "dazzled me and I fancied that I could
master its shape with slight effort." However, a long time
elapsed before he decided to draw the first line, because "the
more I looked over this giant closely, the more unapproachable
it seemed to me, and with every passing minute I became more
ill at ease. Finally, starting at the bottom, I ventured to make
a few strokes. But what I produced was lifeless and meaning-
less. I continued drawing hastily and blindly, deceiving myself,
confining myself to that part which I was drawing at the
moment, and being totally incapable of relating that section

not to mention the shapelessness of the individual bits—to the whole. The form on my paper grew enormously, especially sideways, and when I reached the treetop I found no more space left for it. I had to make it broad and low like the forehead of an ape and force it onto the misshapen mass, so that the edge of the paper was close to the last leaf while the foot of the tree dangled in empty space. When I looked up and finally surveyed the whole thing, a ridiculously grotesque caricature sneered up at me."

"With every passing minute I became more ill at ease"— that's just what you want to avoid. Therefore, you have to begin differently.

You have already studied foliage. (See illustration, page 71.) Now familiarize yourself with the rhythms of the branches (see pages 38-39)—the jagged, blocked-up quality of a fruit tree, the slimness of birches, the beeches' elegant upward flaming, the steep loftiness of the poplars, and the oak's quality of sadly reaching into space.

From the imagination draw several different sorts of leafless
trees on a hill or an island. Look around in nature with more
watchful, attentive senses. Make sketches when you take a
walk and then make a large drawing of an individual tree or
of a group of completely constrasting trees when you get home.
Stick to work right down to the last twigs, for they should not
look like a haystack or a tangle of wires. "All the numerous
twigs and branches should harmonize together into the rhyth-
mic figure of a treetop." (Kornmann)

Enlarged detail from Dürer's engraving "Jealousy," $5\frac{1}{2}''$.

(Above) Pencil drawing by a 17-year-old.

(Left) Woodcut from an old book on trees.

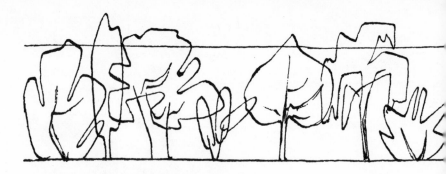

In the summer, trees do not have a transparent effect; they are solid. First study these tree forms two-dimensionally to learn their contours. Take a pencil and divide several sheets into strips of alternating widths about four inches and one inch high. The larger strips can represent the "average height"— for example, a good-sized fruit tree. On the other strip leave space for those treetops which extend above this.

On a walk, draw all sorts of possible tree silhouettes into these strips with your pen, one after the other wherever you happen to find trees and bushes which are clearly visible. You will notice that the silhouettes of the trees usually have a close relation to their leaf forms. Gradually add the main branches and the important interior silhouettes. Start filling them loosely with the appropriate drawing language for the foliage.

However, note that the crowns are not surfaces but solid bodies. Hölderlin writes of the oak: "You seize hold of space with your powerful arm like the eagle its prey, and your sunny crown points strongly and cheerfully towards the clouds." You have perhaps climbed in these treetops and taken refuge under them in the rain. Draw these masses in charcoal both from your imagination and from nature. Draw single trees this way, then groups, and then the edge of a forest. Also see the illustrations on pages 22 and 49.

Plunge deeply into the wealth of tree-trunk forms. These forms are most fascinating near the roots and in the area of

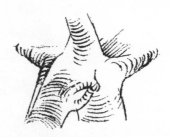

the lowest branches. Beeches are specially recommended for this purpose. From nature you can clarify for yourself with sketches how the roots grow out of the ground and combine to form the trunk. Do the same with the branching out of the limbs by treating them like stovepipes. The most important spot for the roots is where they penetrate the ground; for the branches where they leave the trunk. Finish a large drawing

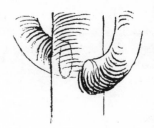

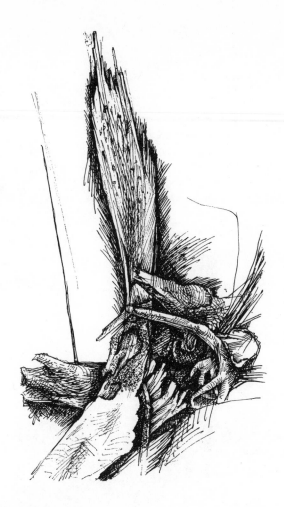

later at home, or start the drawing outside and complete it at home. You can also continue this study in your room with a small branch with twigs—treat it like a full-sized tree. See the illustrations on pages 22, 35 and 111.

95

Both these illustrations are reproductions of large drawings. The original of this drawing is charcoal heightened with white, 15″ high. The original of the drawing on page 97, by the author, is in washed reed pen, 19″ high.

WHAT IS "RIGHT"?

You HAVE ALREADY been reminded several times to create from nature and warned not to copy nature. Obviously when you draw you are concerned with a different kind of "rightness" than that of the photographer who wants to copy. First of all, your drawing is right when it has helped you to see more, when—as Dürer said—you are "internally filled with form." Secondly, your drawing is right when it is unified, when all its parts have something to say, and when they harmonize together in a well-constructed totality, when the chaos of the objects has become a unified configuration. Third, your drawing is right when it expresses some of the essence that has "spoken" to you through the motif's visible form.

All this may frequently be achieved more simply and more purely by drawing from imagination. In drawing from nature, you can easily slip into self-deception. In that case you are drawing the external and not the internal form, what you have seen in front of you and not what you have experienced, the accidental qualities and not the essentials. It is better, therefore, when the object is before you, to *look!* To be sure, you can accompany this looking with sketches to facilitate your concentration.

Goethe said: "Only what I can imagine completely and can redraw from imagination, only that have I truly understood." Even if the object is before you, always draw from imagination. I do hope it is clear that drawing from imagination does not mean drawing from memory and does not mean rummaging in your brain for painstakingly memorized details. In any case, I advise you to begin every exercise with a drawing from imagination. Then observe nature with much closer attention and discover what you lack. I also recommend that after having made a study from nature you draw the same thing again from imagination in order to check what has really become your own—not only your own on paper, but also in your heart.

If you work honestly, without false ambition, and without a mania for dazzling or pleasing others, then the question about the difference between artistic and photographic correctness will answer itself.

POINTERS FOR SELF-CRITICISM

ALTHOUGH THE METHODS and the exercises in this course are the same for all readers, the results are bound to be different. The differences are caused by the different degrees of talent, by a variety of temperaments, and by the different levels of maturity.

"Talent" is a slippery concept. For instance, somebody in the family is held to have great talent and in reality is only a dazzling charlatan, whereas another member makes unpretentious drawings for his own pleasure and is actually the truly gifted one. I gave this book its title deliberately; it was not written for talented or untalented people, but for *willing* people who want to draw along with me and in the process discover the extent of their talent. Everyone has at least a little talent, and that is enough if you cultivate it honestly. Developing your talent is a part of your growth as a human being.

Every sort of *temperament*, every nature, has its advantages and its hazards. A steady hand helps one person attain clarity and strength of line; it leads others astray into routine or misplaced elegance. One person will fall in love with his subject right down to the homeliest details and thereby impart warmth and sincerity to his drawing; another person following this path will get stuck in trivialities and lose sight of the total picture. One person needs constant stimulation by looking at the subject itself; another will be distracted from his true goal by the multiplicity of forms in nature and will take refuge in the haven of copying.

You have to look over your own shoulder and check yourself. Do not try to appear to be more than you are. To copy is to plagiarize nature.

You can also "steal" from your drawing materials. By that I mean, you can "create" some seemingly ingenious charcoal drawings, for example, which are just innocuous, hasty sketches but they are inflated and embellished by the charms of the medium itself. Then the qualities which are really deficiencies tend to be interpreted by others positively, as "artistic" and "impressionistic". However, genuine impressionistic drawing—like Degas' drawing or a Chinese washdrawing—stands at the other *end* of a long road. In such work, nothing at all is formed hastily, superficially or artificially; instead, the fleeting, light qualities which are achieved are just as precise as Dürer's tangible, solid qualities of, say, a tree trunk.

Never draw anything badly because it is too difficult for you. Don't show off; instead, restrict yourself to themes you can cope with. Perhaps you should put the book aside in due time and work longer on this or that exercise.

Where will you find standards? In fine art! Presumably your interest in works of art has grown hand in hand with your own drawing. You will have long since assessed other people's drawings "professionally". Take the best as models and compare your own to them. To be sure, "imitate" them! That does not mean copy them in order to have a facsimile, but rather to re-create what they have done. Don't "forge the signature" of the master, his individual, personal manner, or, even worse, his special tricks. Instead, train your eye. Study great drawings with the same exploring eye you use for nature itself. They will create standards for you and will help you to see nature.

Choose models which show things objectively, drawings which do not bear the personal imprint of the artist too obviously. Choose that type which is not too remote from your own way of drawing. You might select, for example, Pisanello, Schongauer and their contemporaries, and Dürer (especially the copperplate engravings); however, not Grünewald, Rembrandt, or Matisse.

The third reason for differences in drawings is the different levels of *maturity* of different artists. The next group of exercises requires something more than the preceding ones: the creative ability to gather up many individual details into a totality— an ability which not everyone has. A certain type of person should stop here; that is, the type of person who, in music, might prefer a song for one or two voices to a complicated choral arrangement by Bach.

When one is on the right track, creating something, then every stage becomes a goal in itself, for each stage brings development and enrichment with it. Frequently, pressing forward too impetuously is harmful.

Try rendering a landscape, even a bustling crowd of people with individual objects clearly set off against each other. Probably you have seen this done in mediaeval paintings or in a relief on the doors of a romanesque church. It may have seemed odd to you, if your eyes were spoiled by photography. But now, after your own attempts, you perhaps understand these paintings and statues better. What you formerly considered a deficiency, you now recognize as something especially valuable.

There are stages and levels like this for every type of rendering—linear emphasis of directional forces, the tonal chiaroscuro, and the three-dimensional. The illustrations in this book intentionally show both simple and complicated solutions of the same problem side by side.

Here we have reached the boundary of what a book can achieve with "long-distance teaching". "Art is a creation for the eye" (Britsch), and it can only be hinted at with words. I hope that with illustrations and words I have shown you, at least to some extent, a path leading to genuine creativity.

These two drawings of the same motif were done by students the same age who were sitting next to each other. But in spite of this, neither one let the other disturb or influence him. (The one above is pen, the one below, brush.) Such genuine, simpler solutions which correspond to the levels of maturity are also shown by the illustrations on pages 67, 75, 80, 86 and 87.

FROM PRELIMINARY STUDY
TO FINISHED PICTURE

IN DRAWING LANDSCAPES you will be faced with a new problem, and before this you should concern yourself with questions of composition. Even if you were not aware of it, such questions have already been touched upon once—at the beginning in the games on the drawing surfaces and with the different formats. This new exercise consists of unifying the details. Create a unity out of both the blank white spaces on the drawing surface and the parts covered with drawing, just as you would do with the details of the drawing itself. You can practice this in doing a very simple task—such as laying out the address on an envelope.

Study the composition of paintings. Ask yourself questions when standing in front of a well-composed picture. What format is used? What is the proportion of height to width? What is the central object? Where is it situated? How is it related to the format? What are the main directional forces? the minor ones? How are the shades of light and dark distrib-

uted? Where are the dark spots concentrated? the light spots?
How are the edges of the picture drawn into the picture itself?

Answer these questions for yourself while looking at a fairly
uncomplicated picture. Check your understanding of a composition by re-composing its basic features from imagination.
Then repeat this process of re-creation in front of the picture
itself.

Do you sense how all the parts of a good picture are involved
with each other, not just placed side by side? Do you feel the
organized unity with its inner tension? Do you understand how
the empty space "carries" the meaning and why it does not
"float" and is not just stuck in any old place? Do you know the

The marginal sketches around this painting, "Winter Landscape" by Edward
Munch, show how the artist started the composition of his picture with the theme.
It is an idle question whether Munch did all this consciously; he had learned how
to do it. In any case, in order to gain certainty in composition and to train your
eye, you have to clarify this procedure for yourself step by step.

difference between a slice of nature and a picture? For example, the organization of a picture may be simple when the theme is located in the middle. (It will be best for you to compose simply like this at the outset.) Or the organization can be surprising and daring, as in the illustrations on pages 85 and 111, where the central object is pushed dangerously far from the middle towards the upper right or left hand corner. However, the result always has to be a totality, a unity.

Try to learn from this practice how to place even a simple drawing on the surface correctly. If your first attempts do not succeed right away, or if after a time, you have not thought it out well, there is still a chance to make up for the mistake by cutting down the sheet.

LANDSCAPES

LET'S START AGAIN by comprehending the totality of the subject. A landscape is merely a gigantic spectacle. An abundance of forms seems to stretch out and rob you of your courage. Where and how can you start without having something worse happen to you than Green Henry's experience with his tree?

On a walk in the country, when a "melody" which moves you separates itself from this immense abundance, when a certain view fascinates you more than all the rest, stop and observe it for a long time. Seek out the essential things in the terrifying multitude of mountains, hills, trees, houses and paths. Go over this with your eyes even before you begin to draw. What says something special, what is the central object? And at the same time, also ask yourself: in what format can that best be rendered—long and broad? narrow and high? or in a restful square?

Take the landscape as you see it for a starting point to "write a poem" about it. Some part of the immense abundance of phenomena around you is supposed to become a *picture*, a condensation of the multiplicity and not a fortuitous slice of it. Therefore, don't use a "view-finder"—it has the opposite effect; it makes a cut-out and isolates. However, you can certainly limit the extent you want your picture to cover by framing it first right and left, and then top and bottom, between the palms of your hands. For example, notice the proportions of the width of the lake to that of the picture, or of the height of a hill to that of an important tree.

Here is an example: A view of a lake between hills. The blindingly bright light surface of the water lies there, cut off in the background by the hills beyond the shore. The horizontal spreading out of the water is forcibly emphasized and intensified by an agitated foreground of diagonal slopes and perpendicular poplars. The three-part theme consists of the horizontal brightness, the vertical dark spots, and the rolling slopes of the borders in intermediate shades. The lake is the central object, so you choose a long rectangular format.

Another example: A view in a glen. Steep rocky cliffs open towards the top to several black tree trunks in the middle of the picture. The upper and lower limits are defined by the 45-degree slope of the path below and by the small tree branches above. The dark verticals in the middle form the central point, so you choose a tall vertical format.

Try to render such sketches in linear pen drawings, then in clearly graduated tones with brush and charcoal, or three-dimensionally with pencil, pen, or charcoal. The more you have practiced this, the more quickly you will progress later. Draw from nature, and draw these sketches again from imagination.

As the next exercise, study the most important single forms, those of the earth: hills, valleys, and the paths cut into them. The beginner tends to look too hastily towards the top with buildings and street scenes, and he also forgets what it is that "carries" everything in a landscape, the ground. As Dürer warned: "You're not supposed to run right up to the top and take a thing by surprise." Gravel pits and quarries are appropriate subjects. Draw them clearly, solidly and graphically. Redraw the abrupt breaks, the overhangs, the resting horizontals, the outjuttings and the slopes with directional hatching. Pretend that an invisible volcanic force has pushed all the elevations of the ground up out of the surface of the earth

and that a giant's hand carved out the valleys and defiles.
Draw gravel pits as if they were Alpine landscapes.

After you have tried this with a pen or pencil, but without
a preliminary pencil sketch, use your brush and a black or dark
brown color, tempera being preferable to water color. Do not
just daub the color on with the brush, but create the forms anew
with all their inner tension: the water lying there peacefully,
the roundness of the tree trunks, and the cover of grass and
earth extending over a precipice.

Enlarged detail from Dürer's engraving "Nemesis," 5″.

Now something can also finally be said about perspective. In the first illustrations on page 56, the forms are seen from above in one view and from below in another. If you were to hold a box exactly at eye level, then you would see the "side view". If you hold it higher or lower, you would have the second or third picture respectively. Now imagine that you are standing on level ground some distance from a house. Then you would see a side view of it. If you were standing higher or lower than the house, then you would have the second or third illustration respectively.

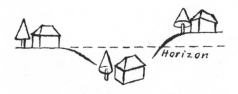

These three ways for an object to appear can occur simultaneously, for example, in a street scene. They then become the controlling factors for a so-called representation in perspective. This has not been mentioned until now, for it will hardly cause you any difficulties at this time. The most important rules are:
Objects become smaller the farther away they are.

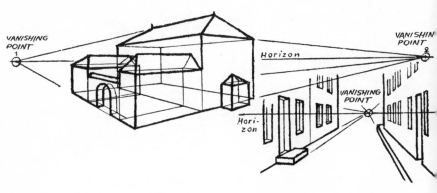

The important line is the horizon, the horizontal line at eye level.

Vertical lines remain vertical.

Horizontals do not run parallel, but always towards their respective "vanishing points". That is, horizontal lines above the horizon descend towards it and those below the horizon rise. Therefore, widths, heights and distances between objects are "foreshortened". The illustrations show two typical situations. Once you are clear about these rules, you will progress on your own from looking at things.

In very many cases, as on pages 57, 59, 64, 65 and 68, a diagonal view is clearer and more intelligible than a representation in perspective.

CONCLUSION

Now WHEN YOU continue to work on your own, seek out your own subjects, and devise your own exercises. And always remember that you are not a photographic film. For just this reason you should *not* sit still as a mouse. Instead, you have to move either yourself or your subject in order to grasp it from as many sides as possible or in order to see it from a good many different vantage points.

You are not a film and should not measure and reproduce the light and dark surfaces of a phenomenon exactly. Instead, submerge yourself in your subject, love it, and create it anew. You can buy a copy of an object or a landscape, but no other person and no machine can accomplish for you what you experience when you draw. During such an hour of creativity you are really a human being; the expiration of an hour of earthly time has become an hour of eternity. Drawing like this will help you give your life form and value.

You are not a film and must not be passive like a film, but rather active and aware of what you want to do. Never start work without a very definite creative purpose. Ask yourself: What is there about the subject that interests me especially? What makes me want to draw it? What do I want to tell others about it in my language of drawing? What media and what format do I want to use to render it? You need a picture in your heart before you are able to bring a picture from inside yourself onto paper. But then, as Dürer said, "From this, the treasure secretly gathered in your heart will become evident through your creative work. . . ."

APPENDIX

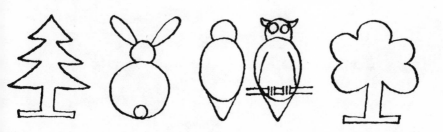

Such illustrations as these are found in the misleading recipe books called something like "Drawing Made Easy" or "Drawing Made Fun". *I advise you to avoid them!* Everything seems easier at first, but soon it becomes more difficult through this method. Such "Drawing Made Easy" actually makes seeing hard. A pattern is forced between the object and the eye of your heart which prevents you from seeing the abundance of the world and from continuing to grow actively in seeing and drawing. What will you have learned from such a method? To copy an empty, expressionless pattern of a tree or an animal, and that's the end of the matter—the end of creative seeing and the end of progress.

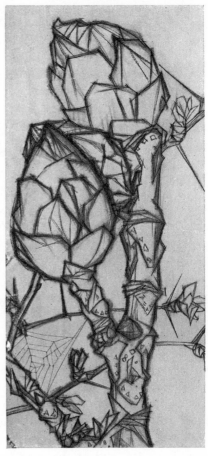

Judging Different Sorts of Work by Means of Contrasting Examples

Compare the illustrations on pages 54, 83 and 84 with these buds. You see here two typical wrong solutions. The sheet on the left was drawn without feeling. The student smacked the taut, swelling buds onto the paper and "shaded" the

stiffly drawn outlines without having experienced the buds and
without having paid attention to their forms, their curves, and
the way they grow out of the branch. What wretched drud-
gery!

The person who drew the illustration at the right "stylized"
it. He adopted a manner just as superficial as the other, but
more striking to the untrained eye, and used it to "throw"
everything onto the paper uniformly. How he chopped up the
branch with his senseless routine tricks!

To be sure, everyone can immediately see how different these illustrations are. The first shows an early Chinese woodcut reproduction of a wash drawing, the second a European

student's work. The first is drawn by a great artist, the second by a dilettante. However, another difference is more important for you: The first is an example of creative drawing of nature, the second a chaotic, formless, copied production. It is not so much a question of whether you ever succeed in drawing such a spendid picture as the first, but whether you are on *this* track and have *this goal* in sight. It is a question of whether you, like that painter, look at the essentials in nature and construct their forms anew on your paper according to your degree of maturity.

What self-deception! In spite of everything, a genuine beginning was made with the tree trunks, the branches, and the little house. But, with the foliage and the water, the person who drew this slipped into senseless copying as well as into "artistic" pretentiousness. Nothing is this easy to come by. What value do such scrawlings have for you or for others? Patience! Have patience! Remember this: before Caesar could call out "veni, vidi, vici" (I came, I saw, I conquered) after a surprising victory, he had been learning his craft a long, long time and had fought, won, and lost many battles.

INDEX

Angular forms, 56-58
Architectural forms,
56-69, 63-66, 69

Ball-point pen, 9
Basic shapes, 12-13
Britsch, 102
Brushes, 9, 12, 29, 34

Charcoal, 9, 27, 28, 34
Chiaroscuro, 41, 69, 102
Composition, 44-46, 53-55, 98,
104-110, 114-115

Da Vinci, 74
Drawing
achieving looseness, 9-10
angular forms, 56-58
architectural forms, 56-59,
63-66, 69
basic shapes, 12-13
composition, 44-46, 53-55, 98,
104-110, 114-115
from imagination, 98-99
fruits and vegetables, 82-83
general rules, 21-23
landscapes, 107-115
linear emphasis, 102
materials, 9, 26-30
matter in space, 48-52
models, 11, 41, 101-102
plants and flowers, 70-81
round forms, 58-63
rules for, 21-23
s-curves, 24-25
textures, 32-34
tonal range, 40-43
with both hands, 19
with the eyes, 47
Drawing leads, 27
Drawing surfaces. See Papers.
Dürer, 46, 98, 110, 116

Erasers, 29

Fixative, 28

Flowers and plants, 70-81
Forms
angular, 56-58
architectural, 56-59, 63-66, 69
in space, 48-52
round, 58-63
three-dimensional, 102
Fruits and vegetables, 82-83

Goethe, 98
Goose-quill pens, 28
Green Henry, 85-86, 107

Hatching, 50, 73
Hölderlin, 92
Holding brush or pencil, 12

Imagination, drawing from, 98-99
Imitation, 101-102
India ink, 29
Ingres paper, 26-27
Inks, 29

Keller, Gottfried, 85-86, 107
Kornmann, 87

Landscape, 107-115
Liebermann, Max, 70
Linear emphasis, 102

Materials, 9, 26-30
Maturity, 102
Mediums. See Materials.
Models, 11, 41, 101-102
Modulation, 41

Papers, 9, 26-27
Pelikan India ink, 29
Pencils, 9, 12, 27, 34
Pens, 9, 12, 28-29, 32
Perception, 44-55, 98-99, 114-115
Perspective, 114-115
Plants and flowers, 70-81
Profiles, 25
Proportion, 44-46

Radiograph pens, 29
Reed pens, 28
Rodin, 47
Round forms, 58-63
Rules
for architectural forms, 63-66, 69
general, 21-23
of perspective, 114-115

S-curves, 24-25
Scheffler, 47
Shading. See Hatching.
Sighting, 45-46
Sketchbook, 27
Socrates, 36
Surfaces, 9, 26-27
Stylization, 119

Talent, 100
Textures, 32-34
Three-dimensional forms, 102
Tonal range, 40-43
Trees, 85-93

Vegetables and fruits, 82-83

Unity, 98, 105. See also Composition.

"View-finding," 66, 107

123